NLP for Weight Loss

Judy Bartkowiak

Paperback ISBN 9781907685927

Published in the UK by MX Publishing
335 Princess Park Manor, Royal Drive, London, N11 3GX
www.mxpublishing.co.uk

Cover design by www.staunch.com

INTRODUCTION

This is a workout for your mind - not your body. So I'm not going to give you a list of all the foods to avoid or tell you to exercise as I'm assuming you know all that and let's face it there are plenty of books around that give you this information. There are also lots of very good diets around and organisations that run classes and weigh you every week and maybe you've tried them. I certainly have. They are excellent and there is plenty of evidence that they are effective.

They don't work for everyone though and they don't always work long term. People lose the weight they want to lose and then what happens? Within months or even years, on it goes again. Not for everyone but for a great proportion certainly. So why do these classes and programmes work better for some people than others? Could it be that it isn't about the programme itself but actually more about us and how we engage with the programme? Instead of comparing the different diets and weight loss programmes and organisations perhaps what we should be looking at instead is ourselves.

You can use this book in conjunction with any other Weight Loss Programme because it is about what's going on in your mind and how you can change it to become the slim person you want to be. It's about raising your confidence so you believe in yourself. It's about valuing yourself and holding true to what you want because the goal is worthwhile, because you are worthwhile. Your mind and body are one. How can you feel good in yourself when every time you look in the mirror a fat person looks back at you? I want you to hold your head high, look at yourself in the mirror and say 'I'm OK'. This 'OK' for you may not be a size ten or even 12, it will be what feels good to you, whatever that size or weight may be.

I want children and teenagers to read it as well because we all need to feel good about ourselves and have self-esteem. In my Therapy Practice (NLP Kids) I've seen so many teenagers who feel bad about themselves and guess what, they are overweight. Losing weight doesn't automatically make you happy or confident although lots of people think that they will be happy when they are the weight they want to be. No, you need to feel confident first. You need to feel good about who you are and set goals that you really desire and value. Once you believe in yourself, then you will lose weight.

This book is based on NLP (neuro linguistic programming) because that's what made the difference for me. Although I have followed different diets over the years, it wasn't until I felt good about myself and who I am, what I've achieved and what I still want to achieve, that I actually committed myself, heart and soul to losing weight because I prioritised ME.

As a working mum, I had always prioritised the family and thought I didn't matter because it was the kids who were important. Then after my first three children left home, I took a long hard look at what had become of the slim young woman I once was and didn't like what I saw at all. I thought quite a bit about who I was as a person, my identity rather than my role in life. I'd always been sporty and fit, yet now I was moving slower, taking the escalators or the lift, avoiding walking and spending far too long sitting at the computer. I thought about the future and how I want to be in my older years and I knew that unless I prioritised myself I wouldn't have the active retirement I dreamed of.

Whatever age you are, I hope you are taking a long hard look at yourself and thinking about making a few changes. One of the changes I would ask you to consider is to read this book and give your mind a work over. I will be asking you to examine your beliefs and the experiences on which they are based. I will ask you to do some exercises, mind exercises, thinking exercises and I'll be asking some difficult questions.

This book isn't about food and exercise for the body it is about food and exercise for the mind, lots of it, but this kind of mind food and drink will make you slim. The reason is because the mind and the body are one. Do the exercises in chapter 1 to experiment with this concept yourself. Then read on and discover how you can make yourself a priority and build your own self-esteem ………and a great new body to go with the new way of thinking.

CONTENTS

ENGAGING NLP

Neuro Linguistic Programming is a way of life, a new and different, positive approach to the way we communicate and how we interpret the way others communicate with us both verbally and non-verbally.

The only way to make effective changes in our life is to engage with this new NLP way and incorporate it daily into everything we do.

At home, at work or at play, whether we are a child, a teenager or an adult, we can make new choices about how we live our life so that we achieve all we wish for in our friendships, relationships and our own state of well-being and happiness.

Engage with NLP and you will see, hear and feel the difference immediately.

HOW TO USE THIS BOOK

Read through each chapter and you'll find lots of exercises
(for the mind) which you can do to integrate the learning.
At the end of the chapter there is some homework which
will move you on in your weight loss journey. There is also
a space for you to record how you are feeling about
yourself having read the chapter and done the homework
and a space for you to record a score out of 10 for how
good you feel about yourself.

Let's start by recording a score before you begin reading
chapter 1. Think about yourself, how you look and feel,
how confident and happy you are with who you are, what
score would you give yourself? Write it in the star here.

You may want to use this space below to record how you feel right now, so you can look back after each chapter and see how far you've moved on. It's very easy, I think, when you're on a mission, to become fixated on where you're aiming for and forget how far you've come already and how well you've done. So let's set a starting point by filling in the space below or if you're visual you may even want to paste a 'before' photo.

Also please remember that this is a programme for the mind so it can be used alongside any diet or exercise regime you are following and it can also be used instead. You will lose weight for sure and you will also feel good about yourself, happier and calmer, confident and full of life.

If you like my workbooks then have a look at the other books in the series:

Engaging NLP for
New Mums
Parents
Children (5-10yrs)
Tweens (10-15yrs)
Teens (15 -20yrs)
Work
Back to Work
Teachers

You can download worksheets, read excerpts and buy online from the Engaging NLP website
www.engagingnlp.com

ABOUT THE AUTHOR

Judy Bartkowiak is an NLP Trainer, Master Practitioner and mother to Lucy, Alex, Jessica and Paul. She is the author of a number of NLP books with a parenting focus and she coaches children, parents, teachers and teenagers from her home in Burnham, South Bucks.

In 2013 whilst ski-ing in Switzerland with her husband and youngest child, Paul, she realised that she no longer had to live through and for her children because the older three had left home and whilst there were of course the phone calls, emails, loans, fridge raids and agony aunt sessions, she could, after 25 years of parenting, prioritise <u>herself</u>.

Despite having written a book on Self-Esteem (Teach Yourself: <u>Self-Esteem Workbook</u>) she realised that her own needs and preferences had always been bottom of the list once everything else and everyone else was sorted out and ticked off. But how often do they all get ticked off? Usually mums crawl into bed at the end of the day thinking about what <u>hasn't</u> been done. So over those 25 years she had become overweight and lazy about herself, she avoided looking in the mirror and although she exercised, it was squeezed in between work, family and home demands and frequently cancelled at the last minute.

She decided that she would give <u>herself</u> some coaching and apply NLP to getting rid of all that excess weight and increasing her exercise by doing things she loved and eating things she liked. She reframed, anchored, set goals, visualised and gave herself resourceful feedback and along with losing weight she actually found she was growing to like herself much more and wanted to treat herself well by eating things that were good for her… because she was worth it. She bought different clothes, smaller sizes – yes, but also brighter colours, more flattering styles and more expensive brands. She enjoyed being in front of the camera rather than forever behind it and noticed bones that hitherto had been covered by flesh.

The process didn't happen overnight, it took more than a year to achieve the size she wanted to be but all the way through the process she enjoyed it, as she gave time to herself and felt good about herself, made decisions that felt good and were not just pragmatic.

Judy is happy to share what she's learned both through this book and in her weight loss coaching consultations via Skype and face to face. She also offers an online email coaching service. If you're reading this prior to returning to work, you may be interested in *NLP for Back to Work*.

Check out the rest of the Engaging NLP series at
http://www.engagingnlp.com

CHAPTER 1
THE MIND-BODY CONNECTION

The premise of this book is that the mind and body are one. How you think affects your body and how you move your body affects how you think. The two parts work together. Here are a couple of great exercises to demonstrate this.

1) Stand and put your right arm straight out in front of you with your finger pointing like this.

2)   Remain facing forwards and move your arm as far around to the side and, if you can, behind you, keeping your arm straight. Now turn round and notice the point you reach with your finger. What are you pointing at?

3)   This time, close your eyes and repeat the exercise and imagine going further round, staying relaxed and comfortable. Now open your eyes and turn around to check how much further you moved your arm.

4)   Repeat the exercise imagining getting another few inches further, again stay relaxed and comfortable.

5)   And another few inches again staying relaxed and comfortable.

6)   Now another few inches.

7)   Open your eyes and see how much further you have managed to reach when you use the power of your mind.

For the next exercise you need someone to work with you.

1) Person A put out your right arm, palm down and just think about what you're going to do tomorrow, normal sort of thoughts, nothing too exciting. This is a control or default for us to compare with.

2) Person B rests their hand on Person A's arm and gently pushes it down. Person A resists.

3) Notice the effort it takes and both give a score 0-10 of how much resistance you felt.

4) Break state. This means you both relax and move around a bit.

5) Now Person A holds out their arm again but this time think of something sad, think about things that haven't gone very well, things you could do better, think about how you feel about being overweight perhaps. Think about it as if it's happening now.

6) Person B rests their hand on A's arm and gently pushes it down with A resisting. What score would you give their resistance this time? I expect it was much easier to push the arm down.

7) Break state again.

8) Now Person A is to think of something that's gone really well recently, something you feel proud of that makes you feel confident and pleased with yourself, perhaps you feel good that you've made a commitment to follow this weight loss book. Again think of it as if it's happening now. Person B again rests their hand on A's arm and tries to push it down, with A resisting. What was the score this time? B, was it much harder to push A's arm down?

Now switch over so you both get to experience the exercise. This is something you can do with children too. Having experienced it once though, the second time may be less remarkable because you both know what happens and may try to influence the result! It will work better if you do the exercise the other way round with a new person who isn't aware of what happens.

Did you find that even though at a conscious level you weren't changing the amount of resistance you were offering up to B, by using your mind, you influence your body? Imagine then that if you can alter your body subconsciously just by a change of state in your mind how you could use this at a conscious level to make specific changes in your body?

Here's another physical exercise to show you how easily you can change what's going on in your body by changing how you think, as if you need more convincing!?

Look up to your left and think about how you looked last week. Imagine seeing yourself, how you looked, what you were wearing, who you were with, what you were doing. Can you picture it? You are gathering remembered images from the past (see the diagram below).

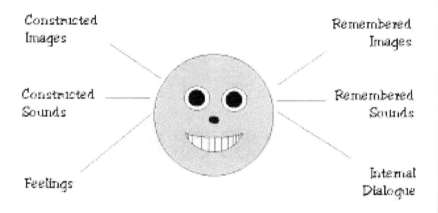

Now look up to the right and think about how you'd like to look , what would you like to be wearing, where would you like to be, with whom? These are your constructed images. If you are left handed these might be the other way around. You can construct the images just as you wish so make yourself look as you'll look when you've lost that weight. Perhaps you've got a special event coming up, a wedding or a christening, a party, a holiday and you have an idea of the clothes you'd like to wear for it. Look up and to the right and picture yourself in those clothes. You may want to imagine the clothes size you will be when you've lost weight. Can you see the label on the clothes, or on the hanger? What size does it say?

You may want to focus on the scales. I know that was my motivation. So remember what horrible numbers showed on the scales in the past or even yesterday, then look up to the right and imagine what numbers you want to see there instead.

If you are more auditory than visual and tend to pay attention to what you hear rather than what you see, then you may want to construct some sounds that you'd like to hear. Imagine your best friend complimenting you on how well you look or your partner telling you that you look sexy and fabulous. Do the exercise by looking to the left to remember what might have been said in the past and then switch to the right and imagine what you want to hear in the future.

Some of us have a very strong internal dialogue going on in our head such as:

Look down and to the left to tell the annoying internal dialogue to be quiet. Tell it what you <u>do</u> want to do instead.

If you're a fidgety kinaesthetic you'll be more conscious of how you feel. You'll be more conscious than most people about the tightness of your clothes and feelings of sluggishness.

Look down and to the right to imagine how much more energy you'll have and how great it will be for your clothes to feel loose when you have lost weight.

Using eye accessing cues like this is a great way for you to be in touch with your body and keep that connection going between body and brain. Use this as part of your new weight loss programme and 'future pace' your day by imagining how well you will eat, what exercise you will do, how you will feel and how great it is to be on the path towards a healthy happy life style.

Do you know the fastest way to feel happier? It is to laugh. When we laugh we move muscles in our entire body, starting with fifteen muscles in the face alone.

Then your respiratory system gets involved as our breathing changes and gradually muscles contract throughout your body. You take in more oxygen so you feel more alive and alert, less sluggish. It is quite difficult to fake laughter and it's difficult to suppress it but when you find something to laugh about you will quickly feel happier and more positive.

Victor Hugo said

"Laughter is the sun that drives winter from the human face"

and this quote here from Norman Cousins must surely convince you to make laughter a key ingredient in your weight loss programme

"Hearty laughter is a good way to jog internally without having to go outdoors."

So your homework for this first chapter of the book is to download whatever films or TV programmes you find funny or dig out those old classics on DVD that you used to laugh at. Aim to have a good belly laugh three times a day for the next week. Seek out friends who make you laugh and look for the humour in every situation.

Yes that's right the homework for chapter 1 is to laugh.

Use this space to write how you feel at this stage of the book, what has worked best and how you feel about yourself. Do it after you've done your homework and before you read Chapter 2.

How confident do you feel now, do you feel a greater sense of self-worth?

Put your score here.

And here are a few jokes to keep you going between the chapters

My fat and I are attached at the hip.

Diets are like learning to ride a bicycle. You might need a little push before you find the right balance and speed. And when you fall down, you can make yourself feel better with an ice cream cone.

As you get older, you become forgetful and start losing things. Everything except weight, which I always find exactly where I left it: around my waist.

I have the physique of Wonder Woman. Sorry, I meant a woman wondering what a physique is.

CHAPTER 2
A WORKOUT FOR THE MIND

In the last chapter we learned how our mind and body are connected and how by changing one, we change the other. John Grinder and Richard Bandler developed the NLP Communication Model to help explain how we process what they called 'external events' and which we call 'life'. Here is the diagram we usually use.

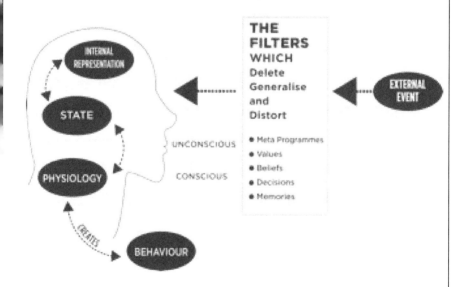

On one side we have an event. Here are a few external events that you might recognise

I see a gorgeous cake……

Or a glass of wine

This could well be the sort of external event that we may be processing. If you are more visual you will be tempted by its appearance because you are more likely to be aware of what you see. You look around a lot and often look up to find images and words in your imagination. Visual processors talk quite fast and have a higher pitch than auditory or kinaesthetic people. The appearance of food will be important, their surroundings need to be attractive and they care a lot about how they look. Visual people tend to use expressions like

"I see what you mean"
"Look at it this way"
"I can imagine"
"I can picture it"
"That's clear"

If you're more auditory and notice what you hear, you'll probably be quite musical, enjoy listening to music, enjoy a good chat and pay attention to the words you use and those you hear. You'll talk slower than a visual person and your tone will also be lower. Auditory people use expressions like

"Let's have a chat"
"I hear what you're saying"
"Can you repeat that"
"That sounds great"
"Tell me more"

They'll be having conversations with others and may also talk to themselves. Maybe someone offers you a glass of wine "Go on, you deserve it after the day you've had." Or maybe you just tell yourself using that beguiling inner voice that "one little cream cake isn't going to matter after all, you're going to the gym, later."

A kinaesthetic person is very animated, doing stuff, moving and fidgeting. They don't talk that much but wave their arms around gesturing and actively expressing themselves. You'll hear these sort of expressions from someone who is more kinaesthetic

"I get your drift"
"Take it from here"
"Get a move on"
"I take that on board"
"It's a struggle"

They are going to imagine how they will feel when they enjoy it, what a great feeling of relaxation or pleasure they will have.

Have you worked out whether you process events in a more visual, auditory or kinaesthetic way?

I process events ....

Think about how knowing this helps you to understand

    a) Your relationship with your partner

    ....

    b) With your children

    ....

    c) At work

    ....

    d) In your weight loss

    ....

....

Now let's go back to the NLP Communication model and find out what happens next.

First we do some **deletion**.

Deletion is when we are selective about what we see, hear or feel, paying attention to what it suits us to pay attention to and deleting everything else. This chimpanzee is deleting what he hears, but we could also be deleting what we see or what we've done.

There will be times when you do something you're not proud of, say something daft, feel embarassed or unhappy with yourself. But when you focus on what you're not happy with, you delete all those other things that make you feel proud and happy. It's really important to experience the whole event and this can be easier if you distance yourself a bit and imagine you're a CCTV camera. Give equal weight to each aspect of the event.

If you're a teenager and you've just had a bad mark, it's OK to feel disappointed but are you deleting that good mark you had yesterday or last week?

In the context of weight loss we could forget that we finished off our child's tea (it doesn't count as a meal does it?!) and then later ate our own. We delete information about the size of the glass perhaps "it's only a small glass" or we delete the number of calories in it, we delete information.

We might also use phrases like this, which are vague and unspecific which delete the detail we need to make sense of the situation.

"Dieting is difficult" – in what way? What aspect? Who says?
"Exercise doesn't help" – help what? What sort of exercise? Who says it doesn't help?
"You have to cut out carbs" – who says? Which carbs? Why?

What do you delete? Examples of ways I delete are

We then **generalise** by making universal truths out of a single event or making a pronouncement and applying it to every situation.

Life is not about how fast you run or how high you climb but how well you bounce.
—Vivian Komori

We say "wine is good for us" or "everyone else is having one, I don't want to be a party pooper". Perhaps we generalise that people on diets are boring or that vegetables are bland or that men have to eat lots of meat.

A classic generalisation is that 'diets don't work' and one I was guilty of 'I don't have time to diet'. I generalised 'time' when in fact there were times when I could fit in some exercise or opportunities such as dog walking when I could have made the exercise more vigorous and effective.

You can recognise a generalisation because you'll hear words like

Everyone
Always
Never
No-one

"I always put on weight on my hips"
"I never have desserts" (I've been known to utter this!)
"I don't drink during the week" (except if I've had a bad day, a friend comes round, we go out...)
"I usually go to the gym three times a week"(well I did one week)

Then there are 'drivers' which are another type of generalisation, such as 'must', 'have to' and 'should'. They suggest you have no choice when in fact you could be more flexible by replacing the driver with the word 'could'.

"I have to cook for the family"- but it could still be healthy
"I must lose weight" – I could lose weight if I wanted to
"I should exercise more" – I could exercise more

The third type of generalisations are called 'stoppers' because that's exactly what they do.

"I can't run to save my life" – who is stopping you? What would happen if you did?
"I won't be able to stick to the diet" – who is stopping you? What would happen if you did?

Start to notice when you use these generalisations and rewind. Reword what you just said or thought (that pesky internal voice again!) and challenge it. Ask

Who says this?
How do they know?
How do I know?
What would happen if I could do it?

Give yourself flexibility. Give yourself choices. The person with the most flexibility controls the system. This is an NLP belief of excellence. John Grinder and Richard Bandler found that successful people had different beliefs from unsuccessful people and they termed them 'beliefs of excellence' and invited us to act as if they are true in order to achieve our own excellence. This phrase means that when we give ourselves choices we can achieve what we want. There are many ways to succeed, numerous possible solutions. It is up to us to be curious and find what will work, our own model of excellence.

What generalisations do you tend to make?

We also **distort** events by making assumptions about them, putting our own meaning to them which may not be intended. In a sense we are mind reading. But we don't know what other people are thinking. When we say "I know why you did that/said that", truly we don't.

Do you torture yourself over what other people think you look like? Do you think because someone didn't say 'hi' this morning that they don't like you? Do you assume they forgot your birthday because they didn't care about you? This is a form of distortion.

Another is value judgements. When we say something about someone with no evidence to back it up such as "She is so confident". She could be or she could just have a great way to pretend, using NLP techniques perhaps!

Another form of mind reading is when you say that one thing is a direct result of something else such as when we say "You make me cross" when it is actually your choice to be cross. Think about it. How on earth does someone deliberately make you cross if you don't choose to be?

Distortions usually have these words in them

That means that…
So….
Therefore…
X made me do it
I had to ……..

Which do you use?

Deletions, generalisations and distortions play with our thought processes making the event mean something specific to us based on our past experiences, beliefs and values.

The other thing we do to external events is to process them through our own particular filters which in NLP we call 'Meta programmes'. You will quickly recognise which you use most often. There are no right or wrong ones but knowing what they are and what you tend to do, gives you options to try another way and get a different result.

Internal/External referencing

Do you take more notice of what other people say than you do of your own opinion? I was aware as I was losing weight that other people were saying things like "you've lost enough now haven't you?" or "you don't need to lose weight". I had to remind myself that their opinion was not important, what was important was how I felt about myself. When we look at celebrities and want to be like them, or admire our slim friends and compare ourselves to them we are being externally referenced. You will always find someone better looking and someone worse looking, decide for yourself what feels and looks right for you.

How important are other people's opinions to you? If comparing yourself with others isn't helping you lose weight ask yourself – "How do I feel about how I'm doing?"

Give yourself a feedback sandwich (these are very slimming, much more so than actual sandwiches which are horrendously fattening).

How well am I doing?
What could I do more of?
What could I do less of?
Overall, how great am I feeling now?!

Past/present/future

Do you live in the past and imagine that what happened before is bound to happen again? Maybe you've tried to lose weight before and it didn't work and this has become a 'fact' for you, that you won't succeed and that history will repeat itself. If you keep dwelling on the past and your 'so called' failures, then use the eye accessing I've shown you and visualise yourself being successful.

Some of us live in the future, "I'll lose weight after the baby" or "I'll lose weight when I go back to work". The behaviour we need to be successful today has been moved into the future. What you want your future to be has to start today. It's no good saying "I'll be good tomorrow". Be good today.

Live in the present and think about what you're eating and drinking right now, how much you're moving around and what more you could do right now to be the shape and size you want to be.

Let's focus on today then. What could you do differently right now that would make a difference?

Choices / Process

Some people like to have a plan for weight loss with a list of what they should be eating and what exercise they should be taking. They don't want to have to think too much about it and they find choices overwhelming. If you are like that, you'll enjoy planning and writing lists and you'll prefer to follow a menu and exercise regime.

If however you like choices and like to consider all your options such as "shall I have a banana or some nuts as a snack now?" or "shall I have fish or chicken for dinner tonight?" then make sure you factor in some choices and remember that all the options need to be things you like eating or doing. It's no use giving yourself a choice between a cream bun and a piece of celery if you hate celery!

How will you structure your diet and exercise plan so you maximise its affect bearing in mind your preference?

Big chunk/Small chunk

No this isn't about chocolate! Some people like to think in concept terms and others want all the detail. For example, a 'big chunk' person will want to focus on 'eating sensibly' whereas a 'small chunk' person will want to know how many calories are in each item of food they eat and how many calories they're expending on exercise. There's no right or wrong here, just as with the other meta programmes it's more about knowing which you tend to prefer so you can find a strategy to ensure weight loss.

If you like detail, then make sure you get all the information you need to make the right choices. If you don't, then you'll need to have a vague idea. Some people do it like this.

Palm of the hand – meat portion around 3oz
Thumb – cheese portion 1oz
Tip of the thumb – high fat portion 1 teaspoon
Handful – snack portion 1-2oz
Tennis ball – fruit or veg portion

Towards/Away from

This is the most important one of all. Are you losing weight because you don't want to be fat or because you want to be slim? Are you choosing a healthier lifestyle because you don't want to be ill? We're going to be setting some goals but I want you to think about focussing on what you do want, not what you don't want. On that note let's have no more

DON'T ....

What <u>do</u> you want, what will you eat, what will you drink and what will you do for exercise. Get the 'don't' word out of your mind, right now.

If I say to you "Don't think about pink elephants" you're thinking about pink elephants aren't you? That's because in order to make sense of the instruction you have to picture a pink elephant. So you've just done what you were told not to do!

One reason why dieting so often fails is because we spend so much energy and attention on what we can't eat and we tell ourselves off for what we aren't supposed to be doing, eating or drinking. Instead let's put our energy and focus on what we want to be achieving, what we can eat and what we want to be doing to get ourselves to the size we want to be. We could also put energy and focus into the other things in our life that are important to us and when we do that and feel happy and confident we will feel good about ourself and not be tempted to comfort eat. People often eat to cheer themselves up because they are unhappy or unsatisfied in a major area of their life such as their job, their studies or their relationship. So, work on getting whatever isn't working at the moment, into shape.

<u>Time to reflect</u>

Having read through the meta programmes and filters and having decided whether you are more visual, auditory or kinaesthetic, what have you learned about how you process external events and how that might impact on your weight loss strategy? What changes will you make right now in your language patterns? That's the 'linguistic' bit of Neuro Linguistic Programming.

Beliefs

The Neuro part of Neuro Linguistic Programming is all about what is going on in our head, the beliefs we hold. The same external event will have a different meaning based on how we were brought up, our experiences and our values.

From this, we create our own internal representation or our version of events if you like. We're going to have a go at this now for ourselves. Think about something that happens fairly regularly relating to losing weight, that you would like to change. It might be a response to something you see, hear or feel so complete the relevant sentence below.

First I see..
First I hear ....
First I feel..

What happens next? Do you only see part of the information (deletion), do you generalise based on what you experience, do you make a meaning from it that it might not have?

I DELETE the fact that

....

I GENERALISE that

....

I DISTORT it to mean that

....

What belief have you formed about it?

My belief about it is that

....

What is important to me (my values) are that

....

My experience is that

....

My internal respresentation of this event is now that

I feel..

I look..

So then I (behaviour)

....

....

And the result is

....

....

I'm assuming that the result isn't what you want at all otherwise you wouldn't be reading this book.

If you always do what you've always done then you'll always get what you've always got. In other words – it's YOU who has to change.

So your homework for this second chapter of the book is to give yourself a feedback sandwich (zero calories and maximum self-esteem points) every day.

How well am I doing?

What could I do more of?
What could I do less of?
Overall, how great am I feeling now?!

Use this space to write how you feel at this stage of the book, what has worked best and how you feel about yourself. Do it after you've done your homework and before you read Chapter 3.

50

CHAPTER 3
ARE YOU A DRAMA QUEEN?

I want to tell you a story. I think you know it already.

Once upon a time, there was a beautiful girl named Cinderella who lived with her father, her wicked stepmother and her two ugly and mean stepsisters. They treated Cinderella very badly. One day, an invitation arrived for a grand ball which would take place in the king's palace but Cinderella's stepmother would not let her go. Instead she had to help them dress for the ball, and curl their hair. They left Cinderella alone at home, very sad and she began to cry.

Suddenly, a fairy appeared and said, "Don't cry, Cinderella. I am your fairy godmother and you shall go to the ball." But Cinderella said, "But what can I wear?" The fairy godmother waved her magic wand and Cinderella's old clothes turned into a beautiful new ball gown. She then touched Cinderella's feet with the magic wand and suddenly she had the most exquisite beautiful glass slippers on them. "How will I get there?" asked Cinderella. The fairy godmother saw six mice playing near a pumpkin in the kitchen. She touched them with her magic wand and the mice became four shiny black horses and two coachmen and the pumpkin turned into a golden coach. Cinderella was overjoyed and set off for the ball in the coach drawn by the six black horses. Before she left, the fairy godmother said, "Cinderella, this magic will only last until midnight. When the clock strikes 12 you must be home."

When Cinderella arrived at the palace, everybody turned round to see who the beautiful new guest was. Nobody recognised her, not even her own family. The handsome prince fell in love with Cinderella and they danced together all night. Cinderella was so happy dancing with the prince that she didn't notice the time. The clock struck 12 and as she ran from the ballroom one of her glass slippers came off and the Prince picked it up.

He wanted to find out who the beautiful girl was because he wanted to ask her to marry him.

The next day, the prince and his servants took the glass slipper and searched for the lady whose foot would fit in the slipper. All the women in the kingdom tried it on but it would not fit any of them. Cinderella's stepsisters tried to squeeze their foot into it to no avail and would not let Cinderella try the slipper on. The prince insisted and it was a perfect fit. They married and lived happily ever after.

Now you have some questions to answer.

Question 1 – Who was the **victim** in this story?

Yes it was Cinderella. Poor Cinderella, put upon, hard done by and at everyone's beck and call. She appeared to have no friends and she was very unhappy with her life. She couldn't stand up to the ugly step sisters and even her father didn't help her out. She was certainly a victim here.

Question 2 – Who was the **persecutor** in the story?

The ugly step sisters persecuted Cinderella, we don't know why and assume they were jealous of her beauty but she did nothing to stop them so they continued to persecute her. We don't know what they were getting out of this; it appears to be control and approval from their mother, Cinderella's stepmother.

Question 3 – Who was the **rescuer** in the story?

There were two rescuers weren't there? The fairy godmother initially enabled her to go to the ball where she then met the handsome Prince who married her and took her away from the sad life she had before.

Do you ever feel like the victim in your own story, unable to live the life you want to live? Perhaps you feel in some way manipulated or at the mercy of your situation, unable to change it? Write a few words here about those feelings of being a victim.

....

....

....

....

....

....

Do you ever behave like the ugly sisters and persecute someone, whether that is your partner, someone at work, your child? Persecuting is when we blame someone else or something else for our circumstances or our feelings. When we harbour jealous, angry, guilty or bad feelings about someone else, we persecute. Write about these feelings here.

....
....
....
....
....
....

What about the rescuer role, do you step in and make things right for other people because you like to feel needed?

....
....
....
....
....
....
....

A Drama Triangle occurs when we behave as the victim, when we don't take responsibility for our feelings or actions (such as eating unwisely) and we feel bad about ourselves ("poor me"). So we look for a rescuer ("poor you") to make us feel better such as a glass of wine or a piece of cake. But being rescued doesn't feel good so we get angry and persecute ourselves until again we become the victim.

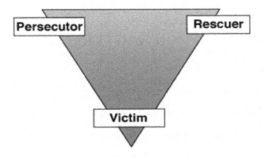

The three roles are co-dependent. The victim needs a persecutor and a rescuer. The persecutor needs someone to pick on and blame, the rescuer needs someone dependent on them and the victim needs to decide not to take any responsibility for themselves.

UNLESS the victim (you) decides to take responsibility and take control of their eating and drinking, learn to monitor what they are consuming, increase their exercise, manage their fitness and say 'NO' to the rescuer . When the rescuer has no role it goes away and is powerless because the power is now with the former victim who has asserted control over their life and takes responsibility for their actions. When this happens the persecutor also fades away because there is no victim there anymore.

Does this situation seem familiar at all?
Think back now to your story. How could you step away from the Drama Triangle? What could you do right now to take control and responsibility so you don't need to be rescued and don't need comfort food or drink?

Now can you think of something else you enjoy doing that would help you to feel good about yourself and that you'd still feel good about tomorrow? What do you enjoy doing, what would be a treat? For many of us parents just having 10 minutes to ourselves can be a real treat so how about some of these ideas.......

Have a nice bubble bath

Paint your nails

Read a magazine or the paper

Chat to a friend

Watch a film

Go for a walk

Put down a few ideas of your own here

....

....

....

....

....

It's important not to be a victim in life; you want to be in control of your life because when you have a child that's what you want for them. When you model having control and being responsible they will learn how to do that for themselves too. If you give in (victim mode) to the temptations of fattening or fast food they will do so too. They will learn the pattern that if you feel down, you eat or drink to cheer yourself up. However, when they see you carving out a little time to treat yourself to some quiet 'me time' or do something you want to do for yourself then that's what they will learn too and this will be very useful at stressful times in their life such as exam time. You don't want them to be turning to food, drugs or alcohol for rescue, you want them to be responsible for their own outcomes including their body shape and size just as you are doing.

So your homework for this third chapter of the book is to take the drama out of your life and take responsibility for your own happiness. Be a Princess and find that bubble bath you got for Christmas, download a book, dig out some nail polish and spend 10 minutes (15 if you can) doing something nice for yourself. Guys – spoil yourselves!

Use this space to write how you feel at this stage of the book, what has worked best and how you feel about yourself. Do it after you've done your homework and before you read Chapter 4.

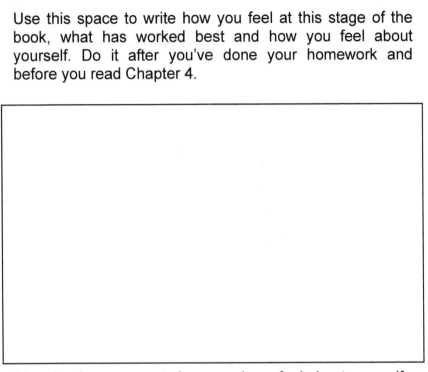

Here is where you note how good you feel about yourself now through treating yourself as a Princess.

CHAPTER 4
SETTING A COMPELLING GOAL

Is it any wonder that the idea of losing weight has such a sense of negativity about it when normally when we lose things we get distressed and go on a mad hunt around the house looking for lost keys, lost phone or hunting on the floor for a lost contact lens (in the grass at a camp site once!). It's not a happy experience is it? When you find what you were looking for, you feel relieved but until then you are desperate and stressed. This is the opposite state we want for becoming the beautiful person we have inside us.

Michelangelo said,

"Every block of stone has a statue inside it and it is the task of the sculptor to discover it."

We haven't always been this size or shape and we aren't always going to be so, what we need to do is discover who we want to be by knocking away like a sculptor to reveal the body we remember or the one we aspire to have.

We can do this by using a **Time Line**.

Imagine a line along the floor and at one end is when you were a child and the other end is old age.

Here is a diagram of how it works

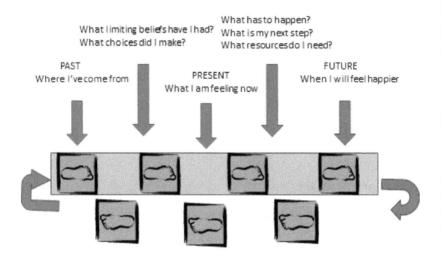

Go and stand at the point that for you represents today (PRESENT on the diagram). As you stand on this spot on the line, think about how you feel about yourself, how you feel right now. This is called 'associating' and it's when we spend time in the 'first person' and really focus on our own thoughts and feelings. For this reason we aren't interested in whether our thoughts are illogical or selfish, this is an indulgent 'all about me' spot. Write down how it feels to be you right now.

....

....

....

So now let's go wandering along the Time Line. Let's travel to a place on it when you felt happy about who you were, how you looked, when you felt confident about your appearance. Go and stand there and notice where you are now, what age, what your situation was, who you were with and what you were doing. Experience it as if it were happening right now. Associate into this time as if it were today, right now. What do you see, what do you hear and what do you feel? Write it down.

....

....

....

....

Do you have a skill in this place on the Time Line that you think would be useful to pick up and take with you back to the 'today' point? If so, let's **anchor** it.

Anchoring is when we set up a conscious association between a really good empowering feeling and an action. Then when we need to use that feeling or state of mind we simply do the action and assuming we've set up the anchor well, then we'll get whatever we have associated with it. So what's the skill or feeling that you have identified that you'd like to put in your kitbag to take back to the present? Think about it long and hard and as you associate, squeeze your earlobe . As the feeling disappears, release the fingers. Give yourself a little shake to 'break state' and repeat the process. If you can, find another example of the great skill or state you're anchoring. Do this three times.

Just to remind yourself – write down the skill or state you've anchored here.

....

....

Now we're off to the future. Head off to a place on your Time Line when you think you'll be super confident and pleased with how you look and who you are. Notice where it is on the Time Line and associate into this place as if it is today. Describe what you're doing, where you are, how you look, what you're wearing even. Maybe you're in a different job, perhaps with a new partner. Be fully associated with what you can see, hear and feel right now in this time in the future as if it's today. Picture yourself there right now and write down what you see.

....
....
....
....

What skill or state of mind do you have that you'd like to gather up from the future to take back to the present? You know what to do. Anchor it as you did with the past. You may want to use a different anchor if it's a different state or skill. Use a thumbs up sign or an OK sign so you have different anchors for different skills or states.

Remind yourself what you've anchored here.

....
....

You should still be standing in the future. Look back along the line to the 'today point'. Do you have anything you'd like to say to the 'you' that was standing there a short time ago, anything you'd like them to know about how the future will be? Say it now.

Which anchor do you think they need to help them? Apply your anchor and slowly walk back with it to the 'today' point. Now you're back to today and with an anchor that you've brought from the future. Maybe you'd also like to add the anchor you applied from your past? So do that one now remembering to break state between anchors. How do you feel now in this today spot. Write it down here.

....

....

....

....

This is a good time to set your goal for the future now you know what future you want for yourself. Write down your goal here

```



```

When we set goals they need to be SMART

Specific – what exactly do you want? Is there a specific size, weight, shape that you want to be or a specific item of clothes you want to wear comfortably? When we are vague and have goals such as "I want to lose weight" or "I want to be fitter", "I want to eat more healthily" we make it difficult for us to achieve it because we don't know exactly what they mean. Some people are OK with such broad brush goals because they can shift the goalposts to suit themselves but this isn't necessarily going to result in achieving the goal. In a sense when we're vague , we are setting up the excuse for not succeeeding. We can say "I just wanted to lose some weight" or "I just wanted to be fitter" and whatever we achieve will sit comfortably there. However, if you want more success than that, you need to be specific and nail your flag to the mast of success. Remember to bear in mind whether you tend to be visual, auditory or kinaesthetic. If you notice what you see and how you look then you may want to make your specific goal reflect that by having a specific visual image. Perhaps there's an outfit you want to get into. I had a client who had a favourite red leather jacket that she wanted to wear again. She hung it on the outside of her wardrobe as a way to remind herself daily of her goal. She's wearing it now!

If you are auditory then perhaps there's someone you want to hear say complimentary things about how you look. Maybe you want to impress your partner or your friends with how great you look? What are the words you want to hear? Say them, write them down somewhere. Make them real.

If you are kinaesthetic then your specific goal may be about how you feel in your clothes. You probably want them less tight around your waist. You may be wanting to feel less sluggish and have more energy. Make this a specific feeling by selecting the item and try it on every week to guage how you're doing. If you want to feel less sluggish, what do you want to feel like? Is there a metaphor for how you'd like to feel? Do you want to feel like a jaguar, a balloon, a kitten?

What is your specific goal?

....

....

....

Measurable – how will you know when you have achieved it?

This is an extension of the first attribute and relates to being able to measure success in terms that can be proven. As well as being specific it needs to be measurable.

....

....

....

Achievable – there is no point aiming for something that is impossible to achieve or undesirable to achieve. We need to do an ecology check to make sure that no-one close to us will suffer by us doing this. If say we set a goal of losing so much weight that it would be detrimental to our health then this is most unwise. Instead, let's agree a sensible goal that we can achieve even if we decide when we have achieved it that we can go on and set another goal afterwards.

....

....

....

Realistic – assuming it could be achieved, is it realistic? Maybe just because it is possible it may not be within your control or you may not be able to do it for another reason for example if you are pregnant, older, just had a baby or something like that. Is yours realistic?

....

....

Timed – we need to set a date for achieving it

....

Now let's have a look at the goal itself.

Is it worded in the positive as a 'towards' goal. That means it needs to be something you want rather than something you don't want. Lots of people talk about weight loss but this is something we don't want. It doesn't help either does it that the very thing you can't have is the thing that you need to be thinking about and planning every day.

FOOD

How would it be if you made a list of all the things that you can eat lots of, that you really like. My list would contain these things: strawberries, raspberries, prawns, lobster, ham, roasted veg, salad, tomatoes, satsumas and quite a lot of other things. What's on your list?

Concentrate on what you can eat not on what you can't eat. Eat them, fill up on them.

I want to ask you some hard truths about your goal now and I want you to be honest.

Why do you want this goal? ....
Why now?...
What's going to be different when you have it?
....

71

What will you be able to do that you can't do now?

....

What won't you be able to do that you can do now?

....

Is that OK?

....

If not ....what are you going to do about it?

....

How much on a scale of 1-10 do you want this goal?

....

Have you ever achieved this goal before? ....

What happened? What will be different now?

....

In order to achieve your goal what strengths and skills do you think you will need? Write a list here

So your homework for this chapter is to focus on what you want. You have spent too long in the past thinking about what you don't want, what you're not and what you haven't got. Now I want you to get your sights firmly on your goal and make it happen.

Use this space to write how you feel at this stage of the book, what has worked best and how you feel about yourself. Do it after you've done your homework and before you read Chapter 5.

Here is where you note how you feel about yourself now through focusing on what you want.

CHAPTER 5
IF YOU THINK YOU CAN'T ....THEN THINK AGAIN

The only thing that will stop you achieving whatever you want in life is YOU!

In the last chapter you worked on setting a compelling outcome, a goal and a vision. Just to remind yourself what it is can you write it here please.

You're going to achieve this goal so let's deal with some of the obstacles that could get in the way.

"I don't deserve to achieve it."

What's that you said? But yes I know what you mean. You are such a low life that you just don't deserve happiness, slimness, fitness, health or whatever you've written in that box.

So I have a few questions for you

Who <u>does</u> deserve it?

....

Why do they deserve it?

....

....

What have they done to deserve it?

....

....

What has to be true for <u>you</u> to deserve it?

....

....

When <u>will</u> you deserve to achieve it?

....

Have you ever deserved it in the past but not now?

....

<u>Who</u> said you don't?

....

When we don't believe we can achieve something, whether it is something as major as losing weight or something minor such as getting to work on time, this belief, the belief that stops us is called a Limiting Belief.

You may recognise it as 'I can't' and it is often accompanied by an 'I can't' physiology which looks like this.

So how do we get these limiting beliefs? Where do they come from?

We often pick them up in childhood when a parent or teacher, someone whose opinion we respect, says "you can't do that" and we carry that into adulthood as part of our identity. If you think your limiting belief has been around a long time, now is the time to get rid of it and decide that you can …..lose weight, be healthy, be fit, stick to a diet …or whatever you want for your goal.

Here's how to do it.

We're going to use something called Perceptual Positioning which is a technique that enables us to understand that limiting belief.

Find three chairs or three cushions and one will represent you and we call that Position 1. Another will be your limiting belief which we call Position 2 and the third is an uninterested bystander or observer who we call Position 3.

Position 1 - You

Position 2 –
Limiting Belief

Position 3 –
Observer

Sit in Position 1 and tell Position 2 what your goal is. Now get up, give yourself a little shake to change state and sit in Position 2. Tell Position 1 why they will not be successful. Remember, in this chair you are the limiting belief, that part of you that says you can't do it. In effect what we are doing here is getting into that mind-set by separating it completely.

Break state again and go back to being Position 1 and tell Position 2 how you feel about them stopping you from achieving your goal. Tell them how you will do it and how you will overturn their attempts to stop you.

Position 2 has a positive intention, it is a part of you and it's there to protect you in some way. Perhaps it doesn't want you to fail and feel bad. Perhaps it is worried you will draw attention to yourself. Only <u>you</u> know this.

Continue to switch positions until you feel you have said all there is to say.

Now go and sit in Position 3 and taking the emotion out of the situation, what did you observe? Do not offer judgements here, just comment on what you saw and heard. Is there some resolution you can suggest?

Go back to Position 1 and decide what you will do now. Write it down here.

....

....

Some people's limiting beliefs may be experienced as blocks or walls, what does yours look or feel like? You can play with this image and give it some colours you like; some soft texture, make it lower, make it out of jelly or ice cream and then it might melt away and let you step over it.

Sometimes we actually put limiting beliefs there ourselves in order to save ourselves from having to do things. What do you get out of saying "I can't" when it comes to losing weight?

....

....

A language pattern that can get in the way of success is when we say "if". For example "If I could run 5km I'd be really proud of myself". How about instead "When I run 5km I will feel really proud of myself"? The word 'if' suggests it may not happen. You are offering yourself a choice.

So what is your homework for this chapter? It is to write a postcard to your limiting belief. Imagine your limiting belief, which is holding you back from what you want to achieve, has gone on holiday. You are writing it a postcard to tell it to stay there and not come back. You are much better off without it and without it you will achieve your goal and be slim, healthy, fit and confident.

POSTCARD

PLACE
STAMP
HERE

FOR ADDRESS ONLY

Use this space to write how you feel at this stage of the book, what has worked best and how you feel about yourself. Do it after you've done your homework and before you read Chapter 6.

Here is where you note how you feel about yourself having rid yourself of those limiting beliefs.

CHAPTER 6.
MAKING A CHANGE

If you always do what you've always done you'll always get what you've always got

Yes we've all heard this expression before haven't we but never was it more relevant than in the area of weight loss. The reason we are overweight is because for years we have been following a pattern that has resulted in the size we are today. We have become accustomed to a certain portion size that is too large for the amount of exercise we take or we are eating and drinking foods that contain far too many calories for the exercise we take. And let's face it, if you are consuming way too many calories then there aren't enough hours in the day to exercise it off, are there?

This chapter is about change. It's about you taking responsibility for change. It's easy isn't it to blame other people. When someone offers you food you don't need or perhaps even want, do you find yourself saying,

"I'll just have <u>one.</u>"
"I'll just have a <u>small</u> portion."
"I don't want to be rude."

"I should eat everything on my plate."

"I'm growing."

"I'll just eat those up to save them going to waste."

"It's so yummy I want to have seconds."

"I don't want to hurt their feelings."

"I deserve it; I've had a bad day."

What are some of the things you say to yourself? Write in the speech bubbles.

It's no good blaming other people for your size because unless they are force-feeding you, it is you who chooses what to put in your mouth.

In order to decide what you need to change let's have a look at the Logical Levels of change diagram.

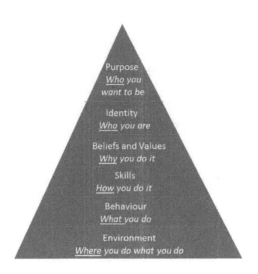

Let's start at the top with your goal that you worked on in the last chapter. Write that in alongside 'Purpose' at the top of the triangle to remind yourself what you're aiming for.

Now let's look at the next level down, Identity. Who are you?

Wow this can be a big question can't it especially if you've recently had a baby or if you've given up work, gone back to work or perhaps you've lost your job. Some women feel an identity crisis when their children leave home and others, when they retire but reflect now on who you are. Find some space on the page to write down what first comes to mind. Your identity might be around how you look, what you do, your hobby or interests, your religion, nationality or whatever is important to you about who you are. We're thinking about words that define you. If you're struggling with this one, think about how your friends would describe you. If someone asked them about who you were, what would they say, what words would they use to describe you that would differentiate you from other friends they have? This isn't really about the role you play but about who you are as a person.

Now let's look at the area of beliefs and values. Firstly values. These are the rules you live by, the things that have to be true for you, that you would if necessary give your life for. So we are talking here about things like freedom, safety, truth, but also the sort of life sayings or quotes that you would describe as your rules for life or mantra. Do you sometimes post these illustrated quotes on Facebook? Maybe you've seen other people's quotes there. Are there any you have seen that you really thought very much reflected your values?

What words or phrases do you use a lot? Are there things you say and your children say "Not that again Mum!" What really annoys you? What sort of behaviour prompts you to lose your rag? The chances are that when you have become very angry or very upset it is because one of your values has been challenged. The last time you felt like that, can you remember why? What value was being compromised? When you have a few values, look at them, and think which of them will be very useful to hang on to in your pursuit of your goal.

Now let's look at your beliefs. These are things you believe to be true at the moment but they change. After all once upon a time you believed in fairies, witches, Father Christmas and so on. You probably believed everything you parents and teachers told you and, who knows, these beliefs may actually have prevented you from achieving what you want in life. Maybe they have even made you unhappy. Now is the time to address some of these beliefs and decide for yourself whether you want them, or not. Make a list of some of the beliefs you hold by completing these sentences.

Some of these sentences may not mean much to you but perhaps you will be surprised at the ones you have completed. Do this exercise without thinking too much because that's how you get close to your beliefs. When you think for a while, logic takes over and doesn't have a place in this exercise.

It is important to look

....

It is important to be

....

People who are slim are

....

Fit people are more likely to

....

When you exercise a lot you

....

People who are overweight are not likely to

....

Losing weight is a good way to

....

The best thing about going out for a meal is

....

Food is one of the …………….…………of my life

When you cook from scratch you can

………………………………………………………………

When you are fat, people think

………………………………………………………………

When I look in the mirror I see a ……………… person

When I am slim I will be ………………………………

The best thing about me is……………………………

When I lose weight my friends will realise that I

am…………………………………………………………

Beliefs change when we have new information. For example when we see father or mother coming in with a sack of presents and discover that after all it isn't Father Christmas we change our belief based on this new information.

Which of the beliefs do you need to change in order to align yourself with your goal. Which belief will be important to keep? Which ones need to go?

Looking at the ones that need to change, what new information do you need in order to change them? Where can you get this?

Can you think of what beliefs you have that will really help you? Write down all the helpful or resourceful beliefs next to that level on the diagram.

The next level down is skills. These are the things you do well. What do you do well that will help you to feel better about yourself, help you to eat sensibly and exercise and all those things that need to happen (you KNOW what they are!). What skills do you need? Write them down here.

Tick the ones you already have and remind yourself of examples of them alongside. Now look at the ones you haven't ticked. Hmm where will we find those? Imagine what your friends and family would say about you. Would they say you had these un-ticked skills? I wonder what they have observed that you just take for granted about yourself. Often things we do unconsciously are the things other people observe and admire without our realising it. So would they tick them, and what examples of those skills might they have observed? Write the most useful skills alongside the level.

The next level down is behaviour. This is what you do. What do you currently do to support the goal you have set? What are your daily actions that work towards your goal? What could you do more of and what could you do less of? Are you willing to make these changes? Check above at your skills and your values and beliefs, does a change in behaviour of the nature you want, fit in with these. We are aiming for you to be aligned so each change at each level needs to fit with the level above and below it.

Lastly let's look at the environment, that's where you do what you do. It's your home, your family, your way of life. What changes at this level need to be made to support the changes you're making at the levels above?

So what is your homework for this chapter? It is to write down all the changes you need to make at each level of the Logical levels pyramid in order to be aligned to your goal. Start making these changes right now.

Use this space to write how you feel at this stage of the book, what has worked best and how you feel about yourself. Do it after you've done your homework and before you read Chapter 7.

Here is where you note how much weight you've lost this chapter through focusing on what you want.

CHAPTER 7
THE WHOLE WORLD IS YOUR GYM

How can you make the most of every opportunity to work your body and let it stretch, exercise and know you love it? If you don't usually do much in the way of exercise, let me introduce you to your body.

Your body does an awful lot of things that you usually won't be aware of such as breathing, picking up your coffee mug, shaking your head, telling you that you need a pee and other communications between your brain and your limbs. One of the things it does as well is that it tells us when we need to eat, when we are hungry and when we need to drink. Mostly we ignore these messages and eat when we want to and instead of stopping when we are full, we carry on.

Sometimes we are triggered by time. It's 11am so it must be time for a mid-morning snack, or its lunchtime so I'll get a sandwich. Other times it could be a colleague mentioning lunch or perhaps you work somewhere where there is a set lunch break. Eating at set times is part of our culture but we don't have to eat like that. When we are aware of our body and what it needs we will make different choices and prepare our food choices in advance so we don't get drawn into making those unwise choices.

So how do we get to know our body so that we open our minds to what it needs?

First, go on, look at it. Take your clothes off and look in the mirror. What do you see? Write down your first thoughts here.

....
....
....
....
....

We aren't very kind to our body and give it a lot of criticism. Is that what you've done? So, now I want you instead to list 10 things you like about your body, any part of it, you choose.

1.
2.
3.

4.

5.

6.

7.

8

9.

10

Now that wasn't so difficult was it?

What is good about those parts that you like?

Do you treat those parts differently to the rest of your body? I know women who are overweight yet they spend hours on their hair and nails and no time at all thinking how they could improve their tummy muscles or tone up their bingo wings. Is that you too?

So what areas would you like to pay more attention to? List them below and alongside each, write down what exactly you'd like to work on. Let's just take three for now.

BODY AREA   WHAT I'D LIKE TO WORK ON

1.

2.

3

Before you start work on any part of your body you need to give it some love. By this I mean – exercise.

Take every opportunity to run up and down the stairs at home and at work. It's even more fun when you clip a pedometer to your waistband so you can see how many steps you've done each day. Aim for around 10,000 as a good average which means some days to get that many you may need to go for a walk. You can make this fun by doing it with a friend, joining a walking group, doing it in a gym class or dance class, or using an exercise DVD or X Box/PlayStation game. Some people like to run, jog or do a fast walk. When I walk I like to occasionally add in some skips or little runs and jumps. Do what you feel like doing and vary it a bit. It's good for the heart to have to work fast for a few minutes then slow it down and then speed it up again. By doing that you're doing a workout for your heart and lungs too. How about making it even more of a lung workout by singing as you run, walk or jog?

I've got a hula hoop and it can be fun trying to get a higher and higher number of hulas. Do it in both directions and you can get some with little bumps on that are supposed to be good for trimming the tummy.

Skipping is really good for a cardiovascular workout so take your skipping rope and get a few minutes skipping in while the kettle is boiling.

Cycling is a great way to exercise and quite a good way to avoid having to look for parking spaces. Combine cycling with taking kids to school and get them into healthy habits, or add some paniers to your bike and do your shopping at the same time.

We need to exercise our upper body too.

Aim for half an hour a day. Now that's not long is it?

After exercise stretch your hamstrings and your calves.

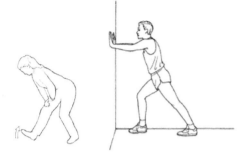

Listen to your body

The more exercise and stretching you do, the more you'll be getting in touch with your body and noticing how well it works and how you can get it to work harder each day.
Now you need to learn to listen to it.
What does it want to eat? What are your favourite foods?
List them here.

Now go back and cross out the things that you don't think your body really wants, not if it wants to enjoy this extra exercise you're giving it. Maybe add on some high energy foods like fruit and nuts, seeds and raw vegetables? Little snack pots of these are great to have on your desk for when you're feeling a bit peckish.

Think about how you could make up some lunch meals that would be super healthy and super delicious. It's generally better to eat more at lunchtime than in the evening because in the evening when you are tired your body will be feeling a bit sluggish and not want to work too hard digesting everything you give it. It's generally considered better to avoid carbs such as potatoes, rice, pasta etc. after 2pm because of this so maybe you could make up pasta salads or rice dishes to eat at lunchtime then stick to just meat or fish and vegetables in the evening.

So your homework for this chapter of the book is to get to know and love the body you have rather than yearn for a different one.

Get going with some stretching and exercises, dig out those old exercise DVDs or buy some from a charity shop, or be creative and use your own playlist and make your own exercise routine. If you're at home with a toddler they'll enjoy joining in. Maybe you can even do your workout to their music! Aim for 30 minutes of exercise a day and it will make a huge difference.

To love your body even more, give it plenty of water;

- *As soon as you get up to rehydrate your body after sleep*

- *Before lunch*

- *Mid-afternoon for rehydration*

- *Before your evening meal*

- *Before you go to bed*

Wait for the rumble before eating. Listen to your body. When your tummy rumbles, eat.

Use this space to write how you feel at this stage of the book, what has worked best and how you feel about yourself. Do it after you've done your homework and before you read Chapter 8.

Here is where you note how good you feel about yourself when you love your body.

CHAPTER 8
THE STRUCTURE OF SUCCESS

What makes NLP unique as a coaching tool is that it focuses on what you do well, what works and how it works. It doesn't go back in time to the past to understand what hasn't worked in the past nor does it offer pat solutions. In this final chapter I want you to focus on the structure of your own success. When you feel good about yourself what are the key factors and what is the underlying belief? So to do that, imagine there is a circle on the floor in front of you. Close your eyes and visualise a time or a day when you felt fabulous, confident, amazing. Imagine it as if it's happening right now. It is a scene from a movie and you are the star.

What do you see?
What do you hear?
What do you feel?

When all those feelings are really powerful, step forward into your imaginary circle and stand there for as long as the feeling is strong. This is called a circle of excellence.

Focus on this belief in yourself and who you are, what you want for yourself in life and your goal or mission. Feel strong and confident that who you are is good and that what you want for yourself is important and of value to you personally.

Whenever you need to get this feeling, step forward into your imaginary circle and get the state.

In this way you get the structure of your own success and by increasing your awareness of when you make good decisions, work well and effectively, make good food and exercise choices you increase the times when you experience the success because you are focusing on it. Where you put your attention is what you will experience more of. This is 'towards' thinking.

You can add to this by learning how others are confident, successful and make resourceful choices that bring them what they want. It is called 'modelling'.

Identify someone who you think has something you'd like in the way of a quality or skill and watch carefully how they do it. Then copy what they do in every detail. Do you get the same result? Possibly not. The reason is because you are still holding on to your own thinking - the thinking that hasn't worked in the past. So if you want a different result you also need their thinking, their belief. You can find this out by asking them about what they believe about the thing they are doing. Now take that belief on and repeat the actions. You may have to delve deeper into the belief because often people don't know how to untangle the innermost beliefs of excellence because it has become embedded in the subconscious.

Once you have the belief that produces the result you want you can try this on yourself by 'acting as if' you have the belief already. Imagine this is your belief. How would you now do this thing with that belief? Do you get the result you want?

The next thing to do is to discover where within yourself you already hold this belief. You may hold the belief in another part of your life, perhaps in your sport, work or socially but once you have identified where you have it you can then anchor it and use that anchor to associate into the belief in this context.

Think about the structure of success. When you achieve what you set out to achieve with the belief that you have just identified, what is the process? What happens first, what happens next? Pay attention to when you make good choices or wise decisions, when are they and in what circumstances?

The person with the most flexibility controls the system. This is one of the NLP beliefs of excellence and it means that when you have a number of options in terms of what to do, you are more likely to have a successful outcome than if you only have one.

This is why this book has offered you a number of techniques. Just to recap, they are:

Anchoring
Circle of Excellence
Time Line
Perceptual Positioning
Visualisation
VAK and the Meta Programmes

Use those that resonate most with you.

Lastly, here are some top tips for at least appearing to be confident as you go through your weight loss journey.

1. Look up
2. Make eye contact
3. Smile
4. Match the other person's language pattern (VAK)
5. Match their pace, volume and way of speaking
6. Match their body language
7. Avoid deletions, distortions and generalisations
8. Focus on what you want
9. Notice when you get it right
10. When you get it wrong, use the feedback as learning

GOOD LUCK!

Judy

Lightning Source UK Ltd.
Milton Keynes UK
UKHW02f1605141217
314463UK00003B/70/P